Francis Frith's
TEES VALLEY AND CLEVELAND

◆

PHOTOGRAPHIC MEMORIES

Francis Frith's
TEES VALLEY
AND CLEVELAND

◆

Maureen Anderson

FRITH
BOOK CO

First published in the United Kingdom in 2000 by
Frith Book Company Ltd

British Library Cataloguing in Publication Data

Tees Valley and Cleveland
Maureen Anderson
ISBN 1-85937-211-2

Frith Book Company Ltd
Frith's Barn, Teffont,
Salisbury, Wiltshire SP3 5QP
Tel: +44 (0) 1722 716 376
Fax: +44 (0) 1722 716 881
Email: info@frithbook.co.uk
Web Site: www.frithbook.co.uk

Printed and bound in Great Britain

Front Cover: Redcar, High Street 1906 54452

AS WITH ANY HISTORICAL DATABASE THE FRITH ARCHIVE IS CONSTANTLY BEING CORRECTED AND IMPROVED
AND THE PUBLISHERS WOULD WELCOME INFORMATION ON OMISSIONS OR INACCURACIES

Contents

Francis Frith: *Victorian Pioneer*

FRANCIS FRITH, Victorian founder of the world-famous photographic archive, was a complex and multitudinous man. A devout Quaker and a highly successful Victorian businessman, he was both philosophic by nature and pioneering in outlook.

By 1855 Francis Frith had already established a wholesale grocery business in Liverpool, and sold it for the astonishing sum of £200,000, which is the equivalent today of over £15,000,000. Now a multi-millionaire, he was able to indulge his passion for travel. As a child he had pored over travel books written by early explorers, and his fancy and imagination had been stirred by family holidays to the sublime mountain regions of Wales and Scotland. 'What a land of spirit-stirring and enriching scenes and places!' he had written. He was to return to these scenes of grandeur in later years to 'recapture the thousands of vivid and tender memories', but with a different purpose. Now in his thirties, and captivated by the new science of photography, Frith set out on a series of pioneering journeys to the Nile regions that occupied him from 1856 until 1860.

Intrigue and Adventure

He took with him on his travels a specially-designed wicker carriage that acted as both dark-room and sleeping chamber. These far-flung journeys were packed with intrigue and adventure. In his life story, written when he was sixty-three, Frith tells of being held captive by bandits, and of fighting 'an awful midnight battle to the very point of surrender with a deadly pack of hungry, wild dogs'. Sporting flowing Arab costume, Frith arrived at Akaba by camel seventy years before Lawrence, where he encountered 'desert princes and rival sheikhs, blazing with jewel-hilted swords'.

During these extraordinary adventures he was assiduously exploring the desert regions bordering the Nile and patiently recording the antiquities and peoples with his camera. He was the first photographer to venture beyond the sixth cataract. Africa was still the mysterious 'Dark Continent', and Stanley and Livingstone's historic meeting was a decade into the future. The conditions for picture taking confound belief. He laboured for hours in his wicker dark-room in the sweltering heat of the desert, while the volatile chemicals fizzed dangerously in their trays. Often he was forced to work in remote tombs and caves where conditions were cooler. Back in London he exhibited his photographs and was 'rapturously cheered' by members of the Royal Society. His reputation as a photographer was made overnight. An eminent modern historian has likened their impact on the population of the time to that on our own generation of the first photographs taken on the surface of the moon.

Venture of a Life-Time

Characteristically, Frith quickly spotted the opportunity to create a new business as a specialist publisher of photographs. He lived in an era of immense and sometimes violent change. For the poor in the early part of Victoria's reign work was a drudge and the hours long, and people had precious little free time to enjoy themselves. Most had no transport other than a cart or gig at their disposal, and had not travelled far beyond the boundaries of their own town or village.

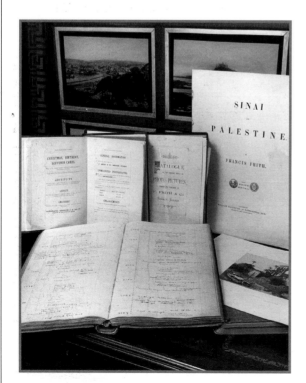

However, by the 1870s, the railways had threaded their way across the country, and Bank Holidays and half-day Saturdays had been made obligatory by Act of Parliament. All of a sudden the ordinary working man and his family were able to enjoy days out and see a little more of the world.

With characteristic business acumen, Francis Frith foresaw that these new tourists would enjoy having souvenirs to commemorate their days out. In 1860 he married Mary Ann Rosling and set out with the intention of photographing every city, town and village in Britain. For the next thirty years he travelled the country by train and by pony and trap, producing fine photographs of seaside resorts and beauty spots that were keenly bought by millions of Victorians. These prints were painstakingly pasted into family albums and pored over during the dark nights of winter, rekindling precious memories of summer excursions.

The Rise of Frith & Co

Frith's studio was soon supplying retail shops all over the country. To meet the demand he gathered about him a small team of photographers, and published the work of independent artist-photographers of the calibre of Roger Fenton and Francis Bedford. In order to gain some understanding of the scale of Frith's business one only has to look at the catalogue issued by Frith & Co in 1886: it runs to some 670 pages, listing not only many thousands of views of the British Isles but also many photographs of most European countries, and China, Japan, the USA and Canada – note the sample page shown above

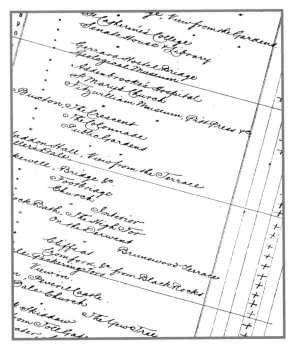

from the hand-written *Frith & Co* ledgers detailing pictures taken. By 1890 Frith had created the greatest specialist photographic publishing company in the world, with over 2,000 outlets – more than the combined number that Boots and WH Smith have today! The picture on the right shows the *Frith & Co* display board at Ingleton in the Yorkshire Dales. Beautifully constructed with mahogany frame and gilt inserts, it could display up to a dozen local scenes.

Postcard Bonanza

The ever-popular holiday postcard we know today took many years to develop. In 1870 the Post Office issued the first plain cards, with a pre-printed stamp on one face. In 1894 they allowed other publishers' cards to be sent through the mail with an attached adhesive halfpenny stamp. Demand grew rapidly, and in 1895 a new size of postcard was permitted

called the court card, but there was little room for illustration. In 1899, a year after Frith's death, a new card measuring 5.5 x 3.5 inches became the standard format, but it was not until 1902 that the divided back came into being, with address and message on one face and a full-size illustration on the other. *Frith & Co* were in the vanguard of postcard development, and Frith's sons Eustace and Cyril continued their father's monumental task, expanding the number of views offered to the public and recording more and more places in Britain, as the coasts and countryside were opened up to mass travel.

Francis Frith died in 1898 at his villa in Cannes, his great project still growing. The archive he created continued in business for another seventy years. By 1970 it contained over a third of a million pictures of 7,000 cities, towns and villages. The massive photographic record Frith has left to us stands as a living monument to a special and very remarkable man.

Frith's Archive: *A Unique Legacy*

FRANCIS FRITH'S legacy to us today is of immense significance and value, for the magnificent archive of evocative photographs he created provides a unique record of change in 7,000 cities, towns and villages throughout Britain over a century and more. Frith and his fellow studio photographers revisited locations many times down the years to update their views, compiling for us an enthralling and colourful pageant of British life and character.

We tend to think of Frith's sepia views of Britain as nostalgic, for most of us use them to conjure up memories of places in our own lives with which we have family associations. It often makes us forget that to Francis Frith they were records of daily life as it was actually being lived in the cities, towns and villages of his day. The Victorian age was one of great and often bewildering change for ordinary people, and

though the pictures evoke an impression of slower times, life was as busy and hectic as it is today.

We are fortunate that Frith was a photographer of the people, dedicated to recording the minutiae of everyday life. For it is this sheer wealth of visual data, the painstaking chronicle of changes in dress, transport, street layouts, buildings, housing, engineering and landscape that captivates us so much today. His remarkable images offer us a powerful link with the past and with the lives of our ancestors.

Today's Technology

Computers have now made it possible for Frith's many thousands of images to be accessed almost instantly. In the Frith archive today, each photograph is carefully 'digitised' then stored on a CD Rom. Frith archivists can locate a single photograph amongst thousands within seconds. Views can be catalogued and sorted under a variety of categories of place and content to the immediate benefit of researchers.

Inexpensive reference prints can be created for them at the touch of a mouse button, and a wide range of books and other printed materials assembled and published for a wider, more general readership - in the next twelve months over a hundred Frith local history titles will be published! The day-to-day workings of the archive are very different from how they were in Francis Frith's time: imagine the herculean task of sorting through eleven tons of glass negatives as Frith had to do to locate a

See Frith at www.frithbook.co.uk

particular sequence of pictures! Yet the archive still prides itself on maintaining the same high standards of excellence laid down by Francis Frith, including the painstaking cataloguing and indexing of every view.

It is curious to reflect on how the internet now allows researchers in America and elsewhere greater instant access to the archive than Frith himself ever enjoyed. Many thousands of individual views can be called up on screen within seconds on one of the Frith internet sites, enabling people living continents away to revisit the streets of their ancestral home town, or view places in Britain where they have enjoyed holidays. Many overseas researchers welcome the chance to view special theme selections, such as transport, sports, costume and ancient monuments.

We are certain that Francis Frith would have heartily approved of these modern developments in imaging techniques, for he himself was always working at the very limits of Victorian photographic technology.

The Value of the Archive Today

Because of the benefits brought by the computer, Frith's images are increasingly studied by social historians, by researchers into genealogy and ancestory, by architects, town planners, and by teachers and schoolchildren involved in local history projects.

In addition, the archive offers every one of us an opportunity to examine the places where we and our families have lived and worked down the years. Highly successful in Frith's own era, the archive is now, a century and more on, entering a new phase of popularity.

The Past in Tune with the Future

Historians consider the Francis Frith Collection to be of prime national importance. It is the only archive of its kind remaining in private ownership and has been valued at a million pounds. However, this figure is now rapidly increasing as digital technology enables more and more people around the world to enjoy its benefits.

Francis Frith's archive is now housed in an historic timber barn in the beautiful village of Teffont in Wiltshire. Its founder would not recognize the archive office as it is today. In place of the many thousands of dusty boxes containing glass plate negatives and an all-pervading odour of photographic chemicals, there are now ranks of computer screens. He would be amazed to watch his images travelling round the world at unimaginable speeds through network and internet lines.

The archive's future is both bright and exciting. Francis Frith, with his unshakeable belief in making photographs available to the greatest number of people, would undoubtedly approve of what is being done today with his lifetime's work. His photographs, depicting our shared past, are now bringing pleasure and enlightenment to millions around the world a century and more after his death.

TEES VALLEY AND CLEVELAND
An Introduction

THE VALLEY HAS a very strong and dramatic industrial past. Iron, then shipbuilding, then chemicals, all helped to make the area a big player on the world market. When the days of heavy industry had passed, as they did in most areas of Britain, the Tees Valley had to look at other ways of keeping its economy going. For a long time this was not an area that the world took notice of, but because it was left to its own devices the Valley had time to build and improve.

Towns and villages are spread out on both sides of the River Tees, which flows from the Pennines through rural and industrial areas on its journey to the North Sea. 'Tees' derives from a Celtic word 'tes', meaning boiling river or river of turbulence; some parts of the Tees, like High Force waterfalls and the rocky rapids of the upper river, show us why it is so named.

The area still has a fair share of heavy industry, but if you think that ugly grey buildings with smoke belching from chimneys is all there is to see, then think again. Ancient market towns, ports, beautiful untouched countryside, historic buildings and sandy beaches are all here, and more. The magnificent backdrop to this patchwork quilt of rural, urban and coastal scenery is the towering Cleveland Hills, which stand silently keeping watch over land and sea. The name Cleveland means 'land of cliffs'.

Sixty or seventy years before the Norman Conquest, land here was given to the diocese of Durham in the time of Aldune, the first bishop, by Styr, son of Ulphus, who was a Saxon. For centuries the bishops of Durham were the ruling

body of a great deal of the area. Eventually, as times and boundaries changed, the area became known as Cleveland. The boundaries have changed again recently; now the area is called the Tees Valley and is made up of five independent boroughs. For over thirty miles the North Sea and the five boroughs go hand in hand. This is not a very large area perhaps, but in that area you will find every different aspect of scenery that can be imagined. The contrasts over the whole region are vast. You can go on coastal walks along sandy beaches, cliff tops and through little fishing villages, and stay at seaside resorts; you can look at churches, old mills and ruins, and learn how our ancestors lived; you can visit industrial towns, which show what man is capable of achieving; you can go on rural walks through lush green countryside, with its ancient hedgerows, dry stone walls and livestock grazing peacefully; all these are monuments to the past and visions of the future yet to come.

The Valley is steeped in history. There have been many noteworthy archaeological finds here; they include Neolithic skeletons, the bones and antlers of deer that have been worked as tools, and many other artefacts, tracing time back to when our ancestors were nomadic, following game over a wide area in their search for food. Ten thousand years ago this landscape was emerging from the ice, and what is now the North Sea was once low-lying fenland. Around this coast,

usually in January or February, certain low tides reveal this ancient forest which once stretched to Scandinavia. Parts of trees and even acorns are clearly discernible, preserved forever in their petrified state. Hartlepool has one of the largest areas of this landscape still visible. Many traces of medieval salt pits or pans still remain, probably the very earliest form of industry; the same process was still being used in the 19th century. There is a record of one of these salt pans that had the curious title of 'Make Beggar'. Many of the place names are a legacy left by the Saxons, Vikings and Normans.

To the Normans, the Tees was the border with Scotland, so throughout the Middle Ages the area was turbulent. One example, which is perhaps partly true and partly conjecture, was when Malcolm III of Scotland harassed the northern provinces: at one point he penetrated as far as Cleveland, and from there went on to Durham, spreading universal desolation. The people fled to churches and other places of worship for safety, but were burned in their imagined sanctuaries. In order to arrest Malcolm's invasion and to make the country no longer an object of his attention, William I 'wasted all the faire countrie betwixt Yorke and Durham, leaving all desolate for three score miles space, which nine years after laid untilled, and with scarcely any inhabitants, when grew so great a famine these northens were forced to eat the flesh of men'.

As time went on and peace settled on the Valley, its people turned to sheep, agriculture and fishing for their livelihoods. The sea was always a rich source of income. In times past, sea coal was collected from the beach to keep the home fires burning; later, the coal was collected and cleaned, then sold to industries to use as pulverised fuel. The many shipwrecks also provided rich pickings - the cargo and timber would often wash up onto the shore. Many an old house has a room panelled out in timber from a wreck. In the late 17th and early 18th centuries, potash and rich sources of iron ore were found, giving birth to heavy industry.

Land had been reclaimed in the past to be used as grazing for livestock. In the 19th century reclamation began in earnest. The Tees Conservancy Commissioners took on the mammoth task of reclaiming the land around the Tees mouth. Slag, the waste from the iron industry that had previously been very difficult and very expensive to dispose of, was used to build walls and divert the Tees to its required course. The sandbanks were removed to make it easier for the ships to sail up and down to the ports, the river bed was dredged, and the silt was used to reclaim the land. Breakwaters were put in place. Prior to this, because of the treacherous coastline and the unpredictability of the weather and the sea, hundreds of ships were wrecked and probably thousands of lives lost, although there is no exact record. Now, with man's intervention, the coast was made much safer for shipping. The reclaimed land was very quickly taken up by industry.

Part of the region's boundary edges the North Yorkshire Moors, which sweep inland to the south-east. North of this boundary lie the villages of Loftus and nearby Boulby; Boulby has the highest cliffs on England's east coast, which rise to more than 650 feet. It also has the deepest mine in Britain, where rock salt and potash are mined at a depth of more than 3,000 feet. Along the coast is Marske-by-the-Sea, where Malcolm Campbell used the beach to practice for the world land speed record. A few miles inland are the two picturesque villages of Kirkleatham and Upleatham. The next coastal town is Redcar, which houses large industrial developments. Magnificent views of the ships steaming in and out of the Tees Port, the second largest port in England, can be seen from here.

To the north west of the Tees, the road passes chemical plants and a nuclear power station to take you into Seaton Carew. This charming resort is a mixture of Georgian, Victorian and modern architecture. The type of visitor here has changed dramatically. In the late 17th and early 18th centuries, the village was a favourite with wealthy Quakers from Darlington. They ploughed an enormous amount of money into the village, including donating the first lifeboat and lifeboat house. There is a beautiful bay, with the town of

Old Hartlepool jutting out on one side; it looks close enough to reach out and touch, even though it is about six miles distant. The other side of the bay is encircled with sand dunes, and in the distance the Cleveland Hills can be seen. The oldest hotel here, built in 1793 on the site of an even older coaching inn called the Ship, is reputed to have a ghost. The ghost was supposed to have been a coachman's wife who was murdered at the old inn. Sometimes a baby can be heard crying, perhaps for its murdered mother!

Hartlepool and Old Hartlepool are classed as two separate parts of the town. Hartlepool was the home of Reg Smythe, creator of the famous Daily Mirror newspaper cartoon 'Andy Capp' - most of his characters were based on people from the town. Old Hartlepool was once a very busy fishing port; the cod from here is still renowned for its flavour. The character of the town has been retained, with its narrow winding streets that were never meant to cater for the motor car. The streets are hilly, which makes it look as though the houses are leaning on one another - perhaps they are! A marina, which has been built on what was once dockland, boasts many attractions including an historic quay, voted one of the six best attractions in England. This is the replica of an 18th-century dockside village. On view is the HMS 'Trincomalee', built in 1817 and still afloat. The 'Warrior' was renovated here before being taken to Portsmouth to be put on show to the public.

Hartlepool's main claim to fame, however, much to the locals' disgust, is the legend of the monkey. The story tells us that during the Napoleonic Wars, a small crowd was on the beach when they spotted a rowing boat, seemingly empty, floating close to the shore. When a fisherman pulled the boat onto the beach, he discovered a creature curled up on the bottom gibbering in fear. He lifted it out and took it to his cottage, intending to give it some food. A little while later, a crowd burst into his home shouting that the creature had been talking French, so it must be a French spy. They dragged the creature, actually a monkey, outside and promptly hanged him. Even now, if anyone says that he or she is from Hartlepool, the question is always asked: 'Where they hung the monkey?'

Storms in years past have caused havoc on the coastline. In February 1838 a violent storm brought waters pouring through the streets of Seaton Carew, nineteen houses in New Stranton were flooded, and a newly-built public house in Haverton Hill was completely demolished. In 1861 more than sixty ships were stranded or wrecked between Hartlepool and Seaton Carew; it was said that you could clamber over the timbers from one place to the other without your feet touching the sand. A partially-built pier at Coatham was never completed because of sailing vessels ramming it and bringing most of the structure crashing into the sea.

There are many lovely little villages tucked away inland just off the beaten track - Greatham, Hart, Elwick, Norton and Longnewton, to name but a few. Greatham is reached by negotiating quite a steep hill. Records of this little parish date back many centuries, and the villagers keep many of the old customs and traditions alive. On Boxing Day at noon, six Morris Men perform the Greatham Sword Dance. Hector is decapitated by the swords of the dancers because he insulted their king; feeling guilty about what they have done, the dancers call the doctor, who revives Hector with a bottle of strong brown ale. The dance continues with the doctor trying to get his fee. The whole village gives one the feeling of stepping back in time.

The best views over town, country and the North Sea are from Eston Nab, once an iron age fort: this high point was crowned with a beacon as far back as the Saxon period, and subsequently it became a ring of beacons to warn of attack from along the River Tees. The beacon was demolished in 1949, and now an obelisk and a plaque recording its history mark the site. From this vantage point an industrial maze of cooling towers, factories and chimneys can be seen side by side with fields. Off in the distance are the white-capped waves of the sea. A natural landscape, and a heritage that is thousands of years old, make the Tees Valley a beautiful and very interesting corner of England.

The Coast

PART OF THE coastline is harsh and rugged, with towering cliffs and rocky coves; then, in sharp contrast, there are long stretches of sandy beaches, secret inlets and sheltered bays, where the waves lap gently at the shore. Whatever the mood of the coast, the scenery is glorious. Just as the coast is so varied, so are the towns and villages that sit upon the cliffs and shores. Most of them were once tiny hamlets depending on fishing for their livelihood. The maritime history of these villages is well recorded in the many museums.

As we travel north, we see the Boulby Cliffs rise dramatically from the sea. Saltburn is a breezy cliff-top resort which is much more sedate than its neighbours. From here, the scenic Heritage Coast runs south-east to Cowbar and into North Yorkshire. The flat sandy beach stretches to South Gare, passing Marske-by-the-Sea and Redcar in its seemingly never-ending length.

On the north side of the Tees, amongst the industry, is Seal Sands bay; here, after more than a century, seals have been reintroduced, and are now breeding. This area is also a haven for birds and wildlife. A mile further on is Seaton Carew, where a new sea wall and promenade have done much to improve the village. When one of the large houses here, now a hotel, was built in 1869, it was said that Staincliffe House 'could soon become an island home with vast water privileges', such were the ravages of the sea before the reclamation of the surrounding land and the building of the breakwaters.

About six miles north, the beaches of Old Hartlepool have a beauty all of their own; they are mainly rocky, with plenty of seaweed and rock pools, a source of treasure trove for the children with their nets, buckets and spades.

SALTBURN-BY-THE-SEA
Skelton Beck 1891
There are many of these little becks and streams meandering down the hills and through the valleys around Saltburn. This one lies at the foot of Cat Nab, a conical hill that separates Skelton Beck from Saltburn Gill. The people in the photograph look rather overdressed to be wading in water. Whatever are they looking for?

◆

SALTBURN-BY-THE-SEA
The Queen's Hotel 1891
The hotel is situated on the upper promenade in 'New' Saltburn, which Henry Pease founded around 1861. He was said to have had a vision of 'a town arisen on the edge of a cliff'. Originally, Saltburn was a hamlet on the shore with about twenty houses and two inns, the Nimrod and the Ship. The people were either fishermen or worked in the alum industry.

SALTBURN-BY-THE-SEA, SKELTON BECK 1891 29205

SALTBURN-BY-THE-SEA, THE QUEEN'S HOTEL 1891 29197

SALTBURN-BY-THE-SEA, THE PROMENADE 1923 74267

This part of the coast was notorious for the smuggling trade. The ravines that ran for miles gave perfect cover for the smugglers to take their goods inland and dispose of them. One well known rogue was John Andrews, who was the landlord of the Ship. In 1827 he was caught by the revenue men and imprisoned. Most of the villagers would have been involved in the illegal trade in some way, either in hiding or buying illicit rum, tea, gin and tobacco.

SALTBURN-BY-THE-SEA, HUNT CLIFFS 1891 29194

This photograph gives a clear idea of the enormity of the cliffs and the breathtaking views that can be seen from them. The remains of a Roman fort was excavated on the top of this cliff in about 1911. Fourteen skeletons were found in the well; all had been brutally killed, showing that this fort came to a violent end. The remains of the fort are now lost owing to erosion of the cliff edge.

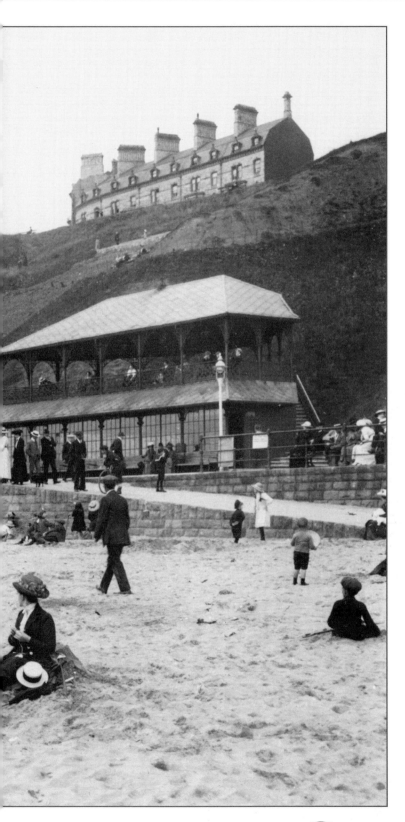

SALTBURN-BY-THE-SEA
THE SANDS 1913 66365
On the left of this view the pier entrance can be seen. When the pier opened in 1869, it was 1,400 feet long, over a quarter of a mile; the length was reduced to 600 feet after a ship, the 'Ovenberg', accidentally rammed into it. Continued storm damage took its toll also. This year, thanks to a lottery grant and other money made available, the pier is undergoing a £2,000,000 restoration; it is hoped that it will be brought back to its former glory and then last another hundred years.

SALTBURN-BY-THE-SEA, THE PIER ENTRANCE 1913 66354
Built in 1884 to save the villagers and visitors the long climb up and down from the village to the lower promenade, this is the oldest remaining working water balance cliff lift in Britain. By the look of the steepness of the steps to the right of the view, one can see why a lift was needed.

SALTBURN-BY-THE-SEA, THE BRIDGE C1885 18109
The Halfpenny Bridge, so named for the toll charge to walk across it, was built in 1869 and spanned the Valley Gardens. In 1974, much to the locals' and conservationists' disgust, the decision was taken to demolish this unusual landmark. Gelignite was spread around the 'legs'. Detonation took place outside the old Toll House on the Saltburn side; in less than four seconds the bridge was destroyed.

MARSKE-BY-THE-SEA
High Street and the Ship Inn 1934 86143
At one time Marske only had two inns: the Anchor on the High
Street, and the Ship on Cliff Terrace. The first Ship Inn closed its
doors in around 1880 and a new public house was built on the
present site in about 1890. Half the building was public and the
other half was a Men's Club. That building was demolished, and
the inn in this photograph was built in 1933. In the present
building there is a stained glass window that was saved from the
previous inn, which advertises the Men's Club.

◆

MARSKE-BY-THE-SEA, ENTRANCE TO VALLEY GARDENS 1938 88395

This view looks along to the High Street and the sea. Most of the houses are still standing, and the peaceful landscaped gardens are still there, but the public shelters and the bandstand were removed many years ago.

MARSKE-BY-THE-SEA, THE OLD THATCHED COTTAGE 1938 88397

Situated on the High Street just across from the Ship Inn, this lovely cottage still remains, although the thatch has been replaced by a modern roof and an extension has been built on one end. At one time these cottages would have been a common sight; many of them were built to house the miners and their families.

MARSKE-BY-THE-SEA, THE CENTRE 1913 66385
In Marton, where Captain James Cook was born, and all through the Tees Valley, there are monuments to this famous explorer. His father was laid to rest in the churchyard of St Germain's on 1 April 1779, just two months after his son met his death in Tahiti. There was no headstone to mark his burial place, just a written record in the parish register.

MARSKE-BY-THE-SEA, REDCAR ROAD 1906 54841
Marske derives from 'mersc' or 'marish', meaning on marshy ground. On Easter Day 1902, a terrible fire broke out in the church of St Mark destroying the roof, clock and tower. The Marquess of Zetland paid to have the rebuilding done.

MARSKE-BY-THE-SEA, THE CHURCH 1906 54848

MARSKE-BY-THE-SEA
The Church 1906
When the church of St Mark was built in 1867, the decision was taken to demolish the old church of St Germain. Legend tells us that as soon as the workmen started to knock down the walls by day, at night 'Hob Men', a type of goblin, built the walls back up again. The authorities eventually had the church blown up with gunpowder to foil the creatures.

◆

MARSKE-BY-THE-SEA
The Church and the Hall 1913
Here we see the parish church of St Mark and Marske Hall at a time when the area was still very rural. The church has a large Norman font that once stood in St Germain's. The font found its way first to a farmyard, where it lay neglected for years; it was then used as a flower pot before being rescued. Then, along with a Saxon cross found in 1901, it was placed in St Mark's.

MARSKE-BY-THE-SEA, THE CHURCH AND THE HALL 1913 66380

MARSKE-BY-THE-SEA
Marske Hall c1885

The hall was built in 1625 by Sir William Pennyman, a loyal Royalist. Because of fines imposed on him by Cromwell's government, he had to sell the hall at a fraction of its worth. Later, the Quaker William Penn, the founder of Pennsylvania, lived there for a while. Later still, it was owned by the Earl of Zetland, who donated it to the Cheshire Homes.

MARSKE-BY-THE-SEA
The Sands 1906

From 1906 until the 1920s, car racing on the beach here was very popular. The sand between Saltburn and Marske was very firm. In 1908 a 60hp Napier Mercury recorded 102 miles per hour. Thousands of people lined the beach to watch these events.

MARSKE-BY-THE-SEA, MARSKE HALL C1885 18126

MARSKE-BY-THE-SEA, THE SANDS 1906 54847

MARSKE-BY-THE-SEA, THE BEACH 1932 85322
The sign at the edge of the slipway forbids motors on the beach. The little hut is used for selling ice cream. This is a very different scene from the one over a century before: in September 1826, the 'Esk', a whaler from Greenland, was wrecked not too far from here. Out of twenty-nine on board, only three were saved -a sad scene for the people of Marske to witness.

MARSKE-BY-THE-SEA, THE SANDS 1923 74148

Looking at this peaceful scene, it seems hard to believe that smuggling was once rife along this coast. A sexton at St Germain's church was caught carrying out the illicit trade. He was killed by the revenue men and buried secretly at midnight. His name was William Stainton. Legend tells that the ghost of Will Watch, Stainton's nickname, haunts the churchyard to this day.

REDCAR, THE TRAFFIC POLICEMAN 1957 K16031

Who would think to capture this scene on camera! This is a wonderful photograph of a policeman doing his traffic duty. He certainly looks well-protected in his box. It brings to mind a metal rubbish bin with the lid raised up on a pole.

REDCAR, QUEEN STREET 1906 54874
There seems to be no shortage of eating places in this street. Looking east, we can see the Trevelyan's Dining Rooms on the corner and Robinson's Albion Tea and Dining Rooms on the left. A general dealer named Smallwood is a real jack-of-all-trades: he advertises petrol, cycles, mail carts, Bath chairs for sale or hire, and CTC repair. The gentleman on the left seems rather suspicious of the photographer.

REDCAR

High Street 1913 66390

The Central Hall is to the right of the clock; until 1861 it was the railway station. In 1873 it opened as Coverdale's market. In the hall there was a jeweller, stationer, printer, gift shop and a draper. The building to the right of the market became the Central Cinema. There is a clear view of the Queen's Hotel. The proprietor at this time was G L Miller.

REDCAR, HIGH STREET 1885 18134
This early photograph shows the wide High Street to the west. The fancy piece of iron work in the foreground is the town's drinking fountain. No 107, on the right, has an unusual title, C Bell, Redcar Ready Money Drapery Establishment. A gypsy caravan trundles slowly up the road towards the fountain.

REDCAR, THE CLOCK c1955 R16046
The building of the King Edward Memorial Clock was discussed in 1902, but the clock was not put in place until 1912, ten years after the King's coronation. The clock was set in motion on January 1913. The Clarendon Arms faces the clock, and the Midland bank is to the left.

REDCAR, HIGH STREET 1906 54451
This view looks east along the High Street. The National Provincial Bank later became the National Westminster. A little further down on the left, between the sun blinds, the large gabled building is the Masonic Hall. On the right the Teeside laundry cart is parked outside the Queen's Hotel - fresh linen today!

REDCAR, NEWCOMEN STREET 1901 48000

This photograph was taken looking north towards the sea. At the end of the street, the pavilions of the Coatham pier head can just be seen in the distance. This street was renamed Station Road in 1935.

[handwritten annotations appear over the caption: "terrace" and "Newcomen tce, and Station road are separate items, and both still exist - see A to Z mfsc S/ro.1 - page 48.38."]

REDCAR, FROM THE PIER 1901 47994

In this view there is a path along the top of the beach; between 1903 and 1904 a new promenade extension replaced the path. Boats were pulled up onto the beach, and fish and shellfish were sold from them. When the level of sand on the beach dropped, the boats were pulled right up onto the esplanade.

REDCAR, FROM THE PIER 1896 37593
The two large buildings are the Royal Hotel, and, on the near side, the Hydropathic Establishment. This was run by Dr Horner, a pioneer in this country in hot and cold salt water baths. The establishment opened in about 1850 with a 'cure for all ills'. The street between the two buildings was Graffenburg Street, named for the first place to use cold salt water in this way. The building eventually became an amusement arcade, and was then demolished to make way for a car park.

REDCAR, THE ESPLANADE 1896 37591
This is a wonderful view of the beach taken during the time of its early popularity. The bathing machines are in use near the pier, and people are sitting in the little boats that are on the sand. The donkeys look busy with their small charges.

REDCAR, THE BOATS 1924 75681
The boat in the centre was named 'Mayflower', and was probably used to take small families on sea excursions. The children are certainly enjoying themselves. There will have been a few pairs of wet knickerbockers when they arrived home!

REDCAR, THE SANDS 1886 18133
While the owners are posing quite happily for the photographer, the donkeys seem a little camera shy. The bathing machines are lined up ready, perhaps waiting for warmer weather. To the east the pier can just be seen in the distance.

REDCAR
THE ESPLANADE 1886 18131
This view looks towards the east. What a peaceful scene as the lady pedals her three-wheeled cycle along the Esplanade. She has probably hired it from the two gentleman sitting talking in the sun while waiting for customers.

REDCAR, THE ESPLANADE C1885 18132

All is calm in this idyllic scene, but the sea was merciless during storms; if sailing vessels were blown too far inland, they had very little chance of not sustaining some damage or becoming completely wrecked. A pioneer lifeboat builder, Henry Greathead, supplied a lifeboat to Redcar in 1802. Still in Redcar, and on view to the public, the 'Zetland' is known to be the oldest surviving lifeboat in the world.

REDCAR, THE BATHING POOL 1932 85320

The pool opened in 1930. A few coppers were charged as the entrance fee, and towels and swimwear could be hired. There was a smaller pool for the little ones next door. In the 1950s the pool closed, and the area became the Rollerdrome skating rink. Eventually this too closed as different forms of entertainment became popular.

REDCAR, THE ESPLANADE 1934 86146

A comedian who performed here named the little park 'Titty Bottle Park', because the nannies from Coatham would wheel their small charges here and use it as a meeting-place. The flower beds were shaped as a diamond, a club, a heart and a spade to represent a pack of cards. The park was eventually done away with because the extremities of the weather so near the coast made it too hard to maintain.

REDCAR, THE PROMENADE 1923 74240
The council acquired the foreshore rights in the early 1920s; the rents for the stalls and kiosks on the beach became too expensive, so the sellers went elsewhere. This seems such a pity, when you can see how busy it was. The Punch and Judy has attracted plenty of attention.

REDCAR, THE PIER 1896 37594
Work started on the pier in 1870; when completed it was over 1,000 feet long. The two entrance pavilions were a toll collector's office and a shop selling buckets and spades. The large sign advertises Robert Conway, Wine Merchant. Ladies' and gents' lavatories were also in the pavilions.

REDCAR, THE SANDS 1906 54447

The pier suffered a catalogue of disasters. It was damaged several times by ships driving into it. In 1899 the bandstand burned down, and then a mine explosion weakened the structure. This, and continuous storm damage, led to its finally being closed. It was sold for the princely sum of £250 in 1980 for demolition.

REDCAR, THE LIGHTHOUSE AT THE MOUTH OF THE RIVER TEES 1925 77751

The lighthouse was built of cast iron and concrete in 1884. Originally lit by paraffin, the light was magnified by lenses and flashed every ten seconds. When the weather was bad, the lighthouse keepers had to get to work with the aid of safety ropes.

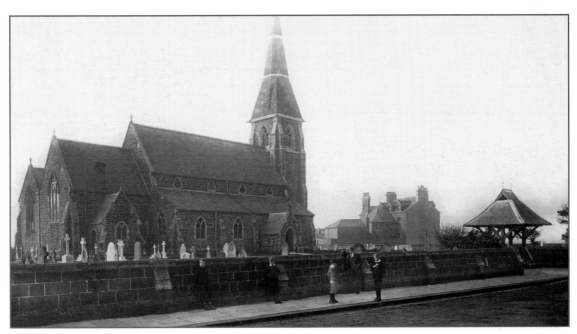

REDCAR, THE CHURCH 1891 29238

Here we see Christ Church in Coatham from the north. Once part of Kirkleatham parish, Coatham became a separate parish in 1854. The church had associations with an Anglican sisterhood that provided medical care in Middlesbrough. Because the church was so solitary, it became known as 'Church in a Field'.

SEATON CAREW, THE GOLF LINKS 1914 67116

In 1874, what was eventually to become known as Seaton Carew Golf Club was founded by Dr Duncan McCuaig, and other lovers of the game, on what is known as Seaton Snooks, a gorse-covered, windswept piece of coastline that was owned by Lord Eldon. This was one of the first fifty golf courses in the world. The military took over the course in the first and second world wars as part of their coastal defences. In 1968 an unexploded mortar bomb, an overlooked relic of war, was found in a bunker.

Seaton Carew, The Sand Dunes c1965 S85036

The fairground, with its many attractions, including a ferris wheel and a roller coaster or 'big dipper', brought hundreds of people to the village. It disappeared in the 1970s. Smaller fairs still set up here in the summer months. A little dune-buggy shoots along just in front of the barn-like building.

Seaton Carew, From the Church c1955 S85014

This is a general view of the south end of the village. Church Street, with its lodging houses and hotel built in 1792, leads onto the front street. On the beach in the distance the fairground can be seen; the roller coaster looks like some sort of sea monster. The trees in the foreground grow in Holy Trinity Churchyard.

SEATON CAREW, FRONT STREET 1903 50000
This view looks south along the street. The Seaton Hotel is the white building with the arched Georgian window. The Oriental Cafe on the left has had many different uses; at one time it was a small cinema. At the present time it is a rather shabby-looking gift shop. On the grass verge nearby is a toddlers' paddling pool.

SEATON CAREW, FRONT STREET 1903 49997
We are looking in the opposite direction to photograph No 50000. The ivy-covered house was called Ashburn; it was demolished in 1923 to make room for a car park for the patrons of the large Marine Hotel next door. The tram line stopped at the Seaton Hotel, because until 1914 a lifeboat house a little further along marked the end of the village. The tram stop was known as Kelly's Corner.

SEATON CAREW, THE PROMENADE c1965 S85023

The promenade has recently undergone a complete reconstruction. It has been extended to the full length of the village, and a sea wall has been erected. The large square area is the North Shelter. The fenced-off land was the roller skating rink. Old Hartlepool can just be seen in the distance.

SEATON CAREW, THE BEACH c1965 S85038

The large house that can be seen on the corner of the Green was built as the George and Dragon Inn in the 17th century. Eventually it was split into two separate residences. One is now the Norton Hotel. During the war the beach was off limits to the public. In 1945 it was reopened, and donkey rides, fairs and stalls reappeared.

SEATON CAREW, THE GREEN 1886 18874

The large house covered in ivy was known as Seaton Hall. It was the residence of Colonel Thomlinson, who was a managing director of Seaton Carew Iron Works when it was a very productive and wealthy company within the iron industry. The house was first built in 1803 as the King's Head Inn. A young girl was hanged on the Green in the 16th century for stealing a loaf of bread, and stocks were still in place here in the 19th century.

SEATON CAREW, THE GREEN c1955 S85007

Seaton Hall became the Seaton Hall Hotel, and then, about ten years ago, a nursing home for the elderly. The ivy has gone, and it now has new bay windows. On the whole, the Green has hardly changed in over a century, and still retains its charming character.

HARTLEPOOL, LOOKING EAST FROM THE FERRY LANDING 1886 18840
The Coal Exchange Hotel is on the right of the picture just behind the ferry terminal. The ferry services were essential to the hundreds of men that travelled to the shipyards and engine works at Middleton. The Commissioner's Ferry was established in 1854.

HARTLEPOOL, THE TOWN WALL 1896 37502
The spire of St Mary's Church can just be seen rising above the rooftops in the distance. Victoria Dock houses the little ferry terminal. Some of the cobles pulled up onto the beach are for hire. The properties along the Town Wall were demolished and semi-detached council housing was built in the 1940s.

HARTLEPOOL
The Lighthouse 1892

This first lighthouse was built in 1847 on what was known as Marine Terrace, now named Cliff Terrace. The lighthouse was dismantled, and a new one built in 1926. The white house nearby was bombarded during the Great War; the two sisters that lived there were killed, and the house was so badly damaged it had to be demolished.

◆

HARTLEPOOL
The Promenade 1901

The promenade was constructed in 1889 as a defence against the ravages of the sea. Large crowds used the facility in their leisure time. A bandstand was provided, and when it was used for shows and entertainment seating could be reserved for 2d.

HARTLEPOOL, THE LIGHTHOUSE 1892   30767

HARTLEPOOL, THE PROMENADE 1901   46955

▼ HARTLEPOOL
ELEPHANT ROCK 1886 18845

Many groups of rocks are hidden underwater around the coast. The Longscar rocks between Seaton Carew and Hartlepool were notorious for damage to shipping. This strange rock formation stood not far out to sea from the Hartlepool lighthouse. On 10 May 1970 it collapsed. At certain low tides its 'feet' can still be seen.

◄ HARTLEPOOL
THE PROMENADE 1903 49995

This photograph shows the bandstand covered in; it could now be used as a dressing room. Whoever these performers are, they must have been popular, judging by the size of the crowd. The lighthouse can be seen in the distance.

East of the Tees

A SHORT DISTANCE inland, on the boundary of the Tees Valley, is Cowbar; then comes Boulby, with its working potash mine. Close by, off the A174, is Loftus. When the ironstone mines were still in production, there was a tunnel which led into the Loftus mines with an opening on the cliff face between Hummersea and Boulby. The miners on their breaks would wave to the fishermen from here. Along the A174 are turn-offs for many little out-of-the-way places, including Skinningrove and Brotton. If you are walking, you can stride down Airy Hill Lane to Skelton Green and then on to Skelton, with its modern community and its ancient castle. Boosebeck, Lingdale, Margrove Park, Lockwood Beck, Moorsholm and Freeborough Hill are all tucked away amongst the hills and valleys that are a backdrop to the moors. Streams and becks cut through the countryside, dividing fields and woodland. Snuggling in at the foot of the moors is Guisborough, with the arch of the medieval priory dating back to the 12th century. A country walk from here is to Commondale via the Quaker's Causeway, taking you through woods, fields and a Bronze Age burial ground.

South-west of Guisborough is Hutton, formerly known as Codhill. The village nestles in a valley in the shelter of tree-lined hills. On the edge of the Guisborough Moor is Roseberry Topping; it appears higher than it actually is, because of the flat ground around it. In the past the mountain was mined for jet and ironstone, but it is now owned by the National Trust, and will remain in its natural state for future generations as a landmark that can be seen for miles. An ancient road leads out above the village onto Percy Cross Rigg to the south-east. The road is believed to have once been connected to the Iron Age fort on Eston Nab and the surrounding settlements.

Heading back towards the river are the villages of Upleatham, Kirkleatham and New Marske. Towards the southern boundary are Normanby and Nunthorpe. Eston lies at the foot of the Eston Hills, which are white with snow in the winter and a riot of pink and purple heather in the summer. Ormesby and North Ormesby are on the edge of Middlesbrough, and are swallowed up in the vast urban development.

LOFTUS
The Mill c1955 L159018
Besides the mines, Loftus had other flourishing trades, such as
tallow candles and wool; in the 19th century, many women were
employed in the manufacture of stays. The women would walk to
Whitby and back in order to purchase the whalebone needed for
their work. It was said that these stays would last a lifetime, and
indeed were often passed down from
mother to daughter.

LOFTUS, CORONATION PARK c1960 L159011

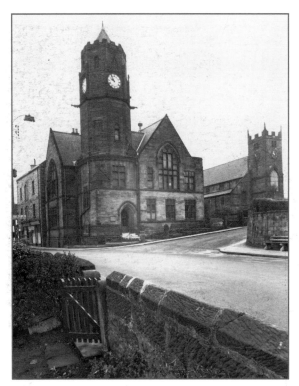

LOFTUS, THE TOWN HALL c1955 L159025

LOFTUS
Coronation Park c1960

To the left can be seen the church of St Leonard, built in 1811 and rebuilt in 1901; it stands on the site of a much older wooden building. All that remains from the original church is a Saxon font that was found in the churchyard. In 1975 St Leonard's celebrated its 700th anniversary.

LOFTUS
The Town Hall c1955

Standing on the south side of the High Street, the Town Hall was built by Lord Zetland in 1869 on the site of the Parish Church School, which dated from about 1746. There is no south-facing clock on the building; funds were running low, and it was cheaper to purchase just three clock faces. The south side was the one most out of sight.

BROTTON, BRITTANNIA TERRACE c1955 B317010

Although Brotton is noted for being a very plain village with the houses built largely of sandstone, the people here have a reputation for their kindness and hospitality, perhaps because their grandparents came from so many different places to seek work in the mines. With the finding of ironstone, the population here grew from 330 in 1861 to 2,672 in 1871. When a south-westerly wind blew, all the candles in the Brotton mine would blow out, leaving the miners in darkness.

BROTTON, SKELTON LANE c1955 B317011

The coach road that came from the Ship Inn in Saltburn to the Brotton railway station was a toll road, which closed once a year to prove ownership. Through its history the village has had feast and famine. In 1920, when there was little demand for ironstone, the miners would lie in bed and listen for the hooter: one blast meant there was work that day, two blasts meant stay in bed, no work.

MOORSHOLM, THE VILLAGE c1955 M323002

Moorsholm means 'a group of huts surrounded by heath'. The village lives up to the title. Today it still remains very much a farming community. Strange earthworks and culverts are still scattered around, relics of a railway that was proposed but never completed. The village is mentioned in both the original and the modern Domesday book.

MOORSHOLM, FREEBOROUGH HILL c1955 M323007

The hill is a landmark that stands on the Whitby to Guisborough road. It was thought that the hill was a burial ground, and man-made because of the symmetrical shape, but geologists have proved that it is a natural feature made up of the same rock and clay as the surrounding areas.

BOOSEBECK, LOCKWOOD BECK c1960 B316005
On early maps this appears as Boos Beck or Goose Beck. This lovely place lies in the hollow of the hills north of Slapewath, the Charltons and Margrove Park. The lake was once underground, covered by a thick layer of sandstone. In 1886, on attempts to sink a mine shaft, water shot into the air and the lake was discovered. Situated off the Guisborough to Whitby road, this is one of the Valley's hidden treasures.

SKELTON, HIGH STREET c1955 S285001
Rather large to be called a village now, Skelton is on the route from Loftus to Guisborough. Not much remains of the original medieval village. There is an old well on Spout Hill, and some ancient stone drinking troughs; on what is left of the village green, there are the remains of the whipping post. In the 1960s and 1970s the village grew considerably to become the larger, friendly community it is today.

SKELTON, THE VILLAGE C1955 S285028

Here we have a general view of the village before modern housing estates, schools and shops were built. This view depicts a very peaceful, rural area, with a patchwork of hedgerows, trees and fields.

SKELTON, THE CASTLE 1891 29207

In the 11th century, a 240 foot moat was dug and the earth was used to form a hill on which a stone castle was built. By 1490 the castle was in poor condition, but even so in the 1700s the owner, John Hall Stevenson, used it to entertain lavishly. In 1788 the castle was demolished, the hill flattened and the moat filled in. In 1794 a Gothic-style castle was built, which is still there today.

SKELTON, THE CHURCH c1885 18125
The old church was pulled down and a new one erected in 1785. The church has a triple-decker pulpit, enclosed pews and a west gallery. After closing in 1904, it stood empty for many years; it has been lovingly restored, and is now back in use.

KIRKLEATHAM HOUSE, THE CHURCH c1885 18136
The history of Kirkleatham goes back many centuries. It was once known as Westlidum, then Lytham; it changed to the present name in the medieval period. In 1623 the manor was bought by John Turner, and the family held the lands until the mid 19th century. The mausoleum was erected in memory of one of the family; it is attached to St Cuthbert's Church, and they are both now Grade 1 listed buildings. The old hall was once a school, and is now Kirkleatham Old Hall Museum.

the smallest church in England.

UPLEATHAM, THE CHURCH 1923 74252

UPLEATHAM
The Church 1923

The church was built in 1684, but the main part of the church was demolished in 1822, leaving this tiny building. There are tablets inside depicting the coat of arms of the Dundas family. By 1966 the church was in a poor state of repair. A company of soldiers from the Green Howards voluntarily restored the building. As a thankyou to them, a plaque was placed inside the church.

◆

UPLEATHAM
The Hospital c1885

This rural village changed dramatically when a rich seam of iron ore was found. Mines were opened in 1851, which employed about 500 men and boys. The mines were said to be the best in the world for producing a high-grade product. The population increased and the village prospered. By 1923 the mines had closed.

UPLEATHAM, THE HOSPITAL c1885 18137

UPLEATHAM, THE HALL c1885 18141

Upleatham began at the foot of the hill; gradually over the centuries the entire village moved up the hill. The laundry from the hall was given by the Earl of Zetland as a school. He paid the headmaster and headmistress an annual allowance. The village had bad land subsidence, and eventually a few of the buildings, including the hall, fell victim to this.

WILTON, THE CASTLE 1891 29240

The original castle, or manor house, was owned by the Bulmer family; it was left to fall into ruin when Sir John Bulmer was hanged and Lady Bulmer burnt at the stake. Her ghost, along with her spaniel, is said to stand on the stairs of the 'new' Wilton Castle, which was built in the Gothic style in about 1806. ICI bought the castle and some of the surrounding land in the 1940s.

WILTON, THE CHURCH 1891 29243

This delightful little village sits at the foot of the Eston Hills just off the A174. The church is Norman; two effigies stand guard in the porch, a knight and a lady. Because of the mining that was carried out here, the land is prone to subsidence; since it is not suitable for large development, it is used mainly for timber and cattle. However, nearby is the large Wilton ICI chemical plant.

GUISBOROUGH, STOREY'S DUMP 1899 44770

This pretty corner of the Valley is on the old Whitby road. The rooftop that can be seen on the right is the old Fox and Hounds Inn; it is still there, but has been modernised. The Storeys were innkeepers in the 19th century, hence the name. In the 18th century there was a mill here. The waterfall runs into the beck which flows into Skelton Beck. A 19th-century bridge is still useable as a link to the old road.

GUISBOROUGH, THE HALL 1907 58664

An extension was added to the right of the hall in about 1902. The original building was a square structure, which was built in about 1857. Lord Guisborough still lives on the estate in the converted stable block, which is now a beautiful house. The hall has had many uses, including an elderly persons' home; there are plans at present for it to become a residential hotel.

GUISBOROUGH, MARKET PLACE 1891 29209

This is a very early view of this ancient market place. The third building on the right was the Cyclists' Club Touring Headquarters. At the end, Jackson's, which sold boots and shoes, must have been well-established, as they were still in business well over fifteen years later. Next to Jackson's was Metcalfe's Newsagents, and on the left is the National Provincial Bank. Are the people posing for the camera, or are they just curious?

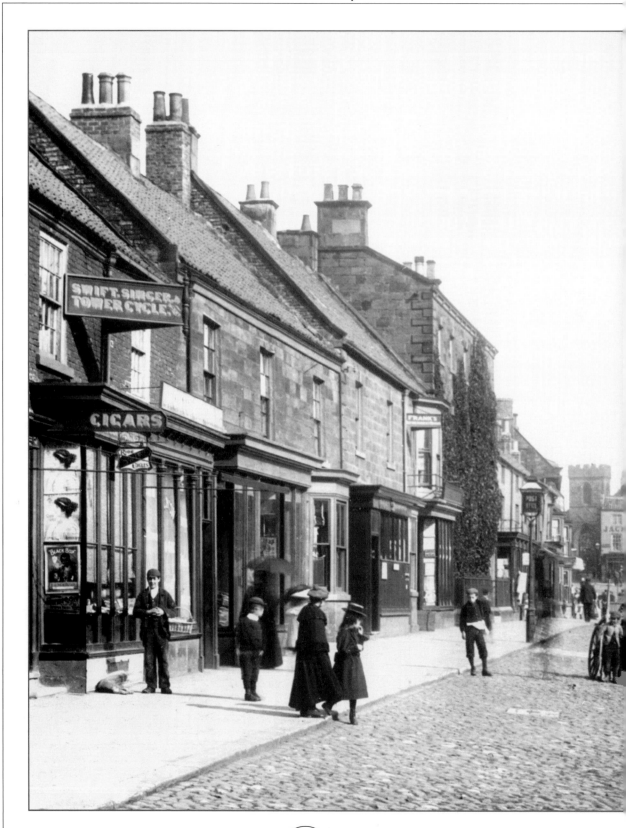

GUISBOROUGH
MARKET PLACE 1899 44758
This view looks east. On the left is Page
the Jewellers, Swift, Singer and Tower's
Cycles, a sign for Frank's, then a post
office. On the right there is a bank that
was converted from the former Cock
Inn in 1875; the archway still exists. The
little boy and girl in the centre look
very protective of each other.

GUISBOROUGH, MARKET PLACE 1907 58660

GUISBOROUGH, THE PRIORY 1885 18151

GUISBOROUGH
Market Place 1907

It is eight years after photograph No 44758 and Jackson's is still there; on the left are a baker and a fish shop, the Buck Hotel and Walter Wilson's. The Market Cross, dating from the early 19th century, was used as a centre for a variety of things. Here scrap and jumble for sale is stacked around. It was also used to break in horses by walking them round and round the cross.

GUISBOROUGH
The Priory 1885

The priory was founded in 1129. Robert de Brus II was a strong patron. The priory was rebuilt twice; all that now remains is this wonderful arch from the 14th century. There is rich decoration in the stonework, including the shields of the patrons. The structure stands a towering ninety-seven feet high.

GUISBOROUGH, THE DE BRUS TOMB 1899 44765

The tomb of Robert de Brus II, an ancestor of Robert the Bruce, King of Scotland, was gathered together in fragments. Some were found at the priory, others at Durham, where they had been taken to use in landscaping, and some were in the church decorating the porch. Pieced together, it now rests in St Nicholas's Parish Church, which is near the priory. There are hopes that a museum can be built at the priory, and the tomb can eventually be placed there.

GUISBOROUGH, HIGHCLIFFE 1913 66020

Situated between Roseberry Topping and Guisborough, the summit is a high point that gives superb views over Guisborough and the surrounding countryside. Highcliffe is marked on the many scenic route maps as an excellent area for walking.

TEESVILLE, ESTON TOWN HALL C1965 T121003
Eston, once a small agricultural hamlet, became home for many miners when iron ore was found. The mine closed in 1949 after over a hundred years in production. A group of cottages built for the miners were known as 'California' - they were named in memory of the American goldrush miners. As can be seen in this photo, nothing remains the same - there are now plenty of modern buildings.

MARTON-IN-CLEVELAND, MARTON HALL C1955 M132019
Built in 1852, the hall stood on the site of what is now Stewart's Park. The hall was built by Henry Bolckow, who was one of the men responsible for the establishment of the iron industry in Middlesbrough. In 1960, the hall caught fire during demolition and was burnt to the ground - a sad ending for such a magnificent building.

MARTON-IN-CLEVELAND, MARTON HALL SHOWING THE COOK MEMORIAL, STEWART PARK c1955 M132016
This view is of the rear of the hall. The land is now owned by the borough council. There is now a conservatory on the site where the hall once stood, and Stewart Park hosts Captain Cook's Birthplace Museum.

HUTTON, HIGHCLIFFE AND THE CLEVELAND HILLS c1885 18145
The hills can be seen for miles from many different locations, but some views are spoilt nowadays by industry rearing its ugly head. In this photograph, the natural beauty of breathtaking scenery is caught forever.

HUTTON, HUTTON HALL 1885 18143

HUTTON
Hutton Hall 1885

Hutton is situated in a narrow valley about 500 feet above sea level. A mine was established here in about 1853. The hall was built by Joseph Pease, a wealthy Quaker, in about 1867. The hall stayed in the Pease family until about 1902. It is regrettable that the hall is now split into flats and has lost its original beauty.

HUTTON
The Village 1891

In 1871 the village was known as Thomas Town. The name changed to Hutton Village in 1880 after Joseph Pease planted many trees to beautify the area. He also built a school for the children of his estate workers, and a mission used as a place of worship. The mission was still in use until well into the 20th century.

HUTTON, THE VILLAGE 1891 29220

HUTTON, THE VILLAGE 1891 29220A
Another boost for this once tiny little place was a railway being built to carry the iron ore from the mine to Guisborough. A station was built at Hutton Gate. The track was built on a stone bridge leading to the village. The station closed in the 1960s.

ORMESBY, HIGH STREET c1955 045001
The Red Lion Inn stands at the back of this view; there is a little newsagent's standing at the end of the row of cottages. The peaceful beauty of this scene has now gone, for the cottages were demolished to make way for a shopping complex.

ORMESBY, ORMESBY HALL C1955 045004

This charming building was bequeathed to the National Trust in 1961 by Colonel J B Pennyman; the family had owned the estates since the 16th century. The hall, which is 18th-century, is now open to the public, and shows what life was like in the Victorian era. The surrounding gardens are a joy to view.

ORMESBY, HARVEST TIME C1955 045005

This scene shows what must have been an everyday sight around most of the villages at one time, but all too rare nowadays. The church of St Cuthbert can be seen in the distance. Ormesby now has spread out so much that it is hard to tell where it ends and Middlesbrough begins.

North-West of the Tees

PICTURESQUE VILLAGES AND towns are all within very close proximity to one another, all are easily accessible and all are worth a visit. Elwick has a tall 19th-century windmill that is used by travellers as a landmark. Oliver Cromwell is mentioned in the parish registers, and a witch, Mother Midnight, lived here in the 16th century and was buried at Hart. Elwick is linked to Dalton Piercy by an ancient bridleway, now a footpath. Billingham, once a hard-working but poor agricultural community, is now a thriving town with a modern, pedestrian-only shopping centre. Thorpe Thewles is surrounded by farmland; its old railway track is now grassed over to make a very pleasant walkway to Castle Eden. Industry once had a place in Norton - the bell for Big Ben's clocktower was made here - but it was never as busy as the other towns, and so has managed to keep a lot of its old-world charm. West from here are Carlton, Redmarshall and Bishopton. Thornaby is a peaceful place, as it is bypassed by heavy traffic. St Peter's church stands silent guard over the village. The wonderful ancient market town of Yarm has a wide main street with mainly Georgian buildings. This was the home of Tom Brown, the hero of Dettingham. John Wesley stayed in a house on the High Street when he came to open the Methodist Chapel in 1768. Yarm also boasts a fine town hall. A short distance away is Teeside Airport.

Travelling through these villages is like a mystery tour: you never know what you are going to come across next. Whether you live here or are just visiting, things can be done at your own pace, the way it has been for centuries.

GREATHAM, THE GREEN c1955 G89008

Greatham means 'village on stony ground'. Many customs are still kept alive in this quaint village. For the Midsummer Feast, a maypole is set up on the Green. The dance was originally a fertility dance performed by adult women, and the records show that many gave birth before the following summer. Even now, the festivities carry on for several days, with many different events taking place.

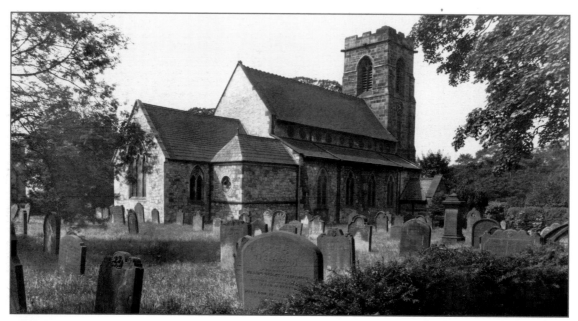

GREATHAM, THE CHURCH c1955 G89002

The church is dedicated to St John the Baptist. Evidence shows that there has been a church on this site since the 8th century. A mouse, the trademark of Thomas Kilburn, the famous furniture maker, is carved on many of the pews. Rebuilt in 1792, the church has since been enlarged. Children crowd here at weddings: another age-old custom of the village is for the newly-weds to throw coins for the children to untie the gates.

GREATHAM, THE HOSPITAL c1955 G89001
The hospital was founded in about 1272, and was dedicated to God, St Mary and St Cuthbert. The hospital was rebuilt in 1803 and was designed by James Wyatt, who also worked on Windsor Castle. Note the beautiful arches to the entrance.

BILLINGHAM, THE TOWN CENTRE c1960 B315063
Billingham is amongst one of the oldest settlements in the Tees Valley, and was a tiny community for over a thousand years. The rural way of life was drastically altered when the Ministry of Munitions acquired a site to the south-east of the village to produce nitrogen for the war effort. Chemical firms later took over the site, and in 1926 it became ICI. These changes made Billingham into the bustling community it is today.

BILLINGHAM, THE GREEN c1955 B315003

Once most of the community here centred around the Green. A man named George Robson (also known as 'Taty' because of his knowledge of potato growing) wanted to build a house along the Green. He was refused permission, so he built upwards instead. His house ended up being sixty feet tall, but with the base of a small room -a real 'folly'. Where has the horse gone? It seems to have abandoned the cart!

NORTON-ON-TEES, THE LYCHGATE AND THE PARISH CHURCH c1955 N69007

North-west of the Green is the church of St Mary, which dates from the late Saxon period. The great cabinetmaker Thomas Sheraton was married here. A legend tells us that to stop church ornaments falling into the hands of the King, they were moved from Durham Cathedral to be taken to Whitby via Norton. Hearing about the fall of Whitby, the carriers buried the treasure to the east of Norton. The site has never been found.

NORTON-ON-TEES, THE POND AND THE VILLAGE GREEN C1955 N69004
Hardly any changes have occurred here; the custodians of Norton's past are determined to protect it for future generations. Norton was lucky in the fact that it escaped the worst ravages of industry. There was a tannery on the Green, and a glue factory in production, but agriculture was always the mainstay of the village.

NORTON-ON-TEES, THE GREEN C1965 N69046
This later view shows the pretty Georgian houses round the Green. Another legend that is still told here is about the hound of Blakestone. By accident he was supposed to have led a pack of hounds to their deaths over the edge of a quarry. The ghost is said to reappear to stop a similar accident ever happening again. Another ghost is the loser of a duel between two soldiers: dressed in a black cloak, the victim appears at the foot of the stairs of the Red Lion Hotel.

CARLTON, BANK LANE c1960 C235004

CARLTON
Bank Lane c1960

Carlton village is situated five miles west of Stockton. The projecting rock at the top of Carlton Bank was extensively worked in the production of alum. A late developer, Carlton remained a rural area well into the 20th century. Many of the buildings are listed. Carlton Bank is 1,338 feet above sea level, and there are some lovely walks in the area with some fine views.

◆

THORNABY-ON-TEES
The Town Hall c1960

Stafford Pottery, a glass bottle works and later, iron works were the industries that moulded Thornaby in the 17th century. In 1962 the local authority bought land here from the Air Ministry to be developed as Thornaby New Town. The Victorian industry is long gone, and has given way to light industry which gives work to thousands of people.

THORNABY-ON-TEES, THE TOWN HALL c1960 T122006

YARM, THE VIADUCT C1955 Y17004

This is one of the largest railway viaducts in England. It was designed in 1849 by Thomas Grainger. There are forty-three arches, and the building of it took over 7,000,000 bricks. Over half a mile in length, it is an impressive feat of Victorian workmanship.

YARM, HIGH STREET C1960 Y17019

Yarm is on a peninsula, with the River Tees on three sides. It was once the main landing place for cargo from the sailing vessels that plied the Tees. The river is now mainly used for angling. The wide High Street takes you north to the oldest bridge in England still in daily use, which dates from circa 1400. The High Street is full of lovely little antique shops.

The Large Towns

TO THE SOUTH-EAST of the Tees is Middlesbrough; its famous Transporter Bridge is a real feat of engineering skill fashioned in iron and steel. The town, built on industry, is very diverse, with people of many cultures; the buildings are a mixture of very old and modern. The existence of the town was due to the Stockton and Darlington Railway, which needed deep water coal staithes; from then on, industry very quickly moved in. In 1818 the population was just forty, but by 1920 it was well over 1,00,000. The town is trying at the present time to be awarded city status.

Stockton was established long before Middlesbrough. When the industrial boom came, thousands of houses were built here to accommodate the workers. On an eleven-mile stretch of the river, where sailing ships once sailed, there is now the spectacular Tees Barrage, a white-water canoeing course that brings thousands of visitors. There is also a replica of Captain Cook's ship the 'Endeavour', which is berthed on the Tees for public viewing.

Darlington is a very busy commercial town; it is the home of the Railway Museum, which houses George Stephenson's Locomotion No 1 and many other famous engines.

Hartlepool Old Town's history dates back to the dawn of time. Here the first soldier to be killed on British soil by German gunfire lies buried. The remains of a wall built in 1315 to keep the marauding Scots at bay can be seen. The ancient church of St Hilda stands silently surveying her domain. Hartlepool centre has a modern undercover shopping complex, and the whole town is seeing vast improvements daily.

MIDDLESBROUGH
North Ormesby Church 1896

Holy Trinity Church, which stands on the corner of Charles Street and the Market Place, was built in 1869. A tower was added in 1880, and the clock in 1883. Once North Ormesby and Ormesby were small communities, but they are now part of the growing town of Middlesbrough.

◆

MIDDLESBROUGH,
Albert Park Promenade 1896

The park was opened on 11 August 1868 by HRH Prince Arthur of Connaught. Henry Bolckow a wealthy industrialist, donated the park to the people of Middlesbrough. It had boating lakes, a maze, a bandstand and facilities to play croquet and cricket. What a lovely way to spend your leisure time.

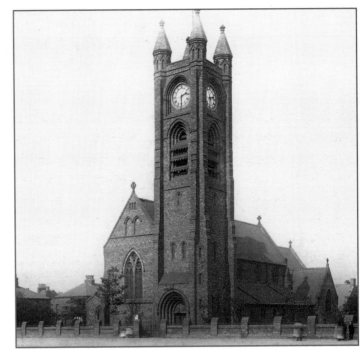

MIDDLESBROUGH, NORTH ORMESBY CHURCH 1896 37569

MIDDLESBROUGH, ALBERT PARK PROMENADE 1896 37576

MIDDLESBROUGH, THE GRAND OPERA HOUSE 1913 66405
Built on the site of a very old farm in 1903 at a cost of £38,000, this venue saw many famous people performing on the stage, including Charlie Chaplin and Gracie Fields. It closed in June 1930 and reopened in March 1931 as the Gaumont Cinema.

MIDDLESBROUGH, THE WESLEYAN CHAPEL 1896 37568
This very imposing building stood on the corner of Coronation and Linthorpe Roads. It was affectionately nicknamed 'Big Wesley' by the townspeople. I wonder if the folk attired in their Sunday best are on their way into the church to listen to two sermons read by the Rev David Wellor as proclaimed on the church board. The chapel was eventually demolished, and British Home Stores took the site.

MIDDLESBROUGH, LINTHORPE ROAD 1913 66411

This view looks south. Opposite Big Wesley is Mansfield Boot Store, advertising 'Any foot accurately fitted'. The corner is a hive of activity: men on ladders appear to be doing some repairs to the front of the store, while another chap is digging a hole at the side of the pavement. There is no traffic about, so perhaps the policeman is there to direct the cycles!

MIDDLESBROUGH, LINTHORPE ROAD c1955 M71004

This more recent view was taken from the junction of Coronation and Newport Roads. Chain stores that are nowadays widespread are pictured here. Burton's are advertising on a plaque that they have a store in New Oxford Street in London, and further down on the left is Boots the Chemist.

**MIDDLESBROUGH
CORPORATION ROAD 1901** 47979
The Town Hall clock tower, 870 feet
high, can be seen on the skyline; in the
distance is the dome of the Empire
Palace of Varieties. The Institute
Building and the Corporation Hotel
are nearly hidden from view as tram No
41 passes in front of them.

MIDDLESBROUGH, CORPORATION ROAD 1901 47980

Here we have a better view of the Empire Palace of Varieties. As with the Opera House, many famous people performed here, including Stan Laurel, George Formby and Marie Lloyd, to name but a few. Seating is for more than 1,000 people. The future of the Empire was uncertain for a time, but in the early 1990s restoration of the building took place.

MIDDLESBROUGH, THE EXCHANGE 1896 37554

The construction of the building, which opened in 1868, cost the Exchange Building Company Ltd £28,000. A 130-foot tower was planned, but it was never built owing to a shortage of money. It was said that the building was the town's finest example of architecture of the period. What a shame that it succumbed to progress and was demolished in the 1980s.

MIDDLESBROUGH, THE MUNICIPAL BUILDINGS 1901 47981
The Town Hall and the Municipal Buildings were the heart of all Middlesbrough's civic affairs. The official opening was in 1883, performed by the Prince and Princess of Wales. This photograph overlooking Victoria Square was taken the same year that the square was opened. It was to become a very popular place with young and old alike.

MIDDLESBROUGH, MARKET PLACE 1896 37559
We are looking south. On the left is the Market Hall and Town Hall, with St Hilda's Church opposite. The first public market here opened in December 1840. It proved so popular that it soon expanded and became quite large.

MIDDLESBROUGH
MARKET PLACE 1913 66408
It is market day and the stalls are set up. There were shooting galleries and other amusements to attract the crowds. In front of the Market Hall is a rag and bone merchant, and at the front on the right is a cart advertising E Peacock Rabbits (in cages).

MIDDLESBROUGH, THE STATUE OF SIR SAMUEL SADLER 1913 66403

MIDDLESBROUGH
The Statue of Sir Samuel Sadler 1913

Samuel Alexander Sadler was a famous industrialist who set up a chemical works in Cargo Fleet Lane. He became Mayor of Middlesbrough in 1910 and died in 1911. He was known as a very well-dressed gentleman who was never seen without a flower in his buttonhole.

◆

MIDDLESBROUGH
The Transporter Bridge 1913

The building of the bridge was discussed in Victoria's reign, but it was not opened until 1901. Pedestrians and vehicles cross by means of a suspended platform which moves to and fro across the Tees.

Whether it is worth the cost of the upkeep has long been a matter of debate. The bridge is often closed for repair, or because high winds make it dangerous to use. On the other hand, it is a symbol of Middlesbrough's industrial past.

MIDDLESBROUGH, THE TRANSPORTER BRIDGE 1913 66412

STOCKTON-ON-TEES, NORTON GREEN 1896 37547

Stockton was once in the parish of Norton; of the two, Norton was the more important. Although Norton has been enveloped by Stockton, it still retains individuality. A weekly market was granted here in 1099. Springs flow under the area, and a dew pond was established by tapping these springs. This remained the main source of water for over 800 years. It was legal to graze cattle on the Green, but not pigs, as they caused too much damage.

STOCKTON-ON-TEES, THE RIVER TEES c1955 S195023

This is an industrial view of Stockton, not very panoramic but a very important part of the town's history. The first iron ship, the 'Advance', was built here by the Stockton Shipbuilding Company. Stockton took trade from Yarm in the boom days, but eventually the trade was lost to the expanding town of Middlesbrough.

**STOCKTON-ON-TEES
HIGH STREET 1896** 37535
At the north end of the High Street the gas lamps are still in place. Steam trams were in use from 1881 to 1897, so although there were tramlines on the road there were no overhead tracks. The almshouses were in this street; they were erected in the 17th century, and were replaced in the early 19th century with accommodation for poor families. The buildings were knocked down in the late 19th century, and the Victoria Building was built on the site.

STOCKTON-ON-TEES
HIGH STREET 1899 44740
The building in the foreground on the right was the Cash Clothing Company. Their slogan was 'The People's Clothing'. Opposite the entrance to Dovecote Street, this end of the High Street was known as Coal Hill because it was where the donkeys, carrying their baskets of coal from Durham collieries, rested. The domed building on the right is the Victoria Building, which was demolished in 1964.

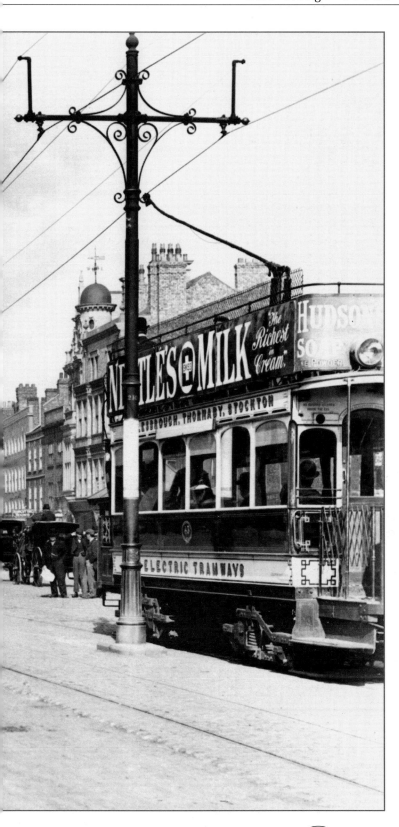

STOCKTON-ON-TEES
HIGH STREET 1899 44738
The flat oblong building in the centre of the street is the Shambles, an indoor market. Behind is the tall pole of the Market Cross, erected in 1768, and the building further back with the clock face is the Town Hall, built in 1735. The hall has had many uses, including a lock-up for law-breakers, a public house and a meeting-place for the town council.

STOCKTON-ON-TEES, HIGH STREET C1955 S195022

In this more up-to-date view, the trams have given way to buses and horses to cars. Even with these changes the street looks much as it did in the 19th century. The market, which dates from 1310, is still held here on Wednesday and Saturday every week. Hundreds of stalls are set up, spanning nearly the width and length of the street.

STOCKTON, GENERAL VIEW 1896 44737

STOCKTON-ON-TEES, THE PARISH CHURCH 1899 44741
The church is known as St Thomas's, but this may be wrong, as it was built in 1710 in Queen Anne's reign, when it was unfashionable to dedicate churches to saints. In 1906 the chancel was rebuilt, and in 1925 the side chapel was added.

STOCKTON-ON-TEES, ROPNER PARK 1896 37545

Still a popular relaxation area, the lake is now planted round with trees, shrubs and lawns. The land was given by the Ropner family, who were amongst the pioneers in shipbuilding in Stockton. The park was opened in 1883 by the Duke and Duchess of York, who later became King George V and Queen Mary.

HARTLEPOOL, MIDDLEGATE c1955 H32015

At the top of Middlegate stands the church of St Hilda. On the right, the Market Hall was replaced by the Borough Hall. In 1929 it housed the Borough Council, the Board of Health, the Magistrate's Court and the Police Station. The central feature is the turreted tower above the entrance. The hall is now used mainly for entertainment.

HARTLEPOOL, NORTHGATE c1955 H32088
This, the old part of Hartlepool, has remained virtually unchanged for centuries. This area has many relics still in existence from the dim past, and is a paradise for archaeologists and historians. Notice the beautiful ornamental lamp at the pedestrian crossing from Cleveland Street.

WEST HARTLEPOOL, CHURCH STREET 1901 46944
A row of hansom cabs await fares. On the right the first building is the new Central Building, built on the site of the Central Hall. The top floor was offices, one of which was used by Lloyds Register of Shipping; there was also a restaurant. On the lower floor there was a tobacconist, a fruiterer, a tailor and a bootmaker. A little further on is the Commercial Hotel. The No 17 tram makes its way eastwards.

**WEST HARTLEPOOL
CHURCH STREET 1914** 67101
The nearest building on the left is the
North Eastern Bank, and on the next
corner is the Yorkshire Penny Bank,
built in 1901. This building was so badly
damaged in a German air raid in 1940
that it had to be demolished. On the
right there was Scott's Corner, and a
little further on was Smithsons.

HARTLEPOOL, CHURCH STREET 1903 49988

The tram crews worked a sixty-hour week with no meal breaks; their wage for a week would have been thirty shillings, the equivalent to about £1.50 now. The tramline was put into Church Street in 1897, the first electric tramway in the north-east to use overhead wiring. The poles, which incorporated lighting, were highly ornamental. The gentlemen look as though they are waiting for a morning tram.

HARTLEPOOL, WESLEY CHURCH 1901 46943

This was built as the Wesleyan Chapel in 1873 at the height of the Methodist influence. This beautiful building stood empty for many years, and there were plans to demolish it and use the land for car parking. However, there was such a strong argument against the idea that eventually the building was restored; it is now a night-club. The building behind is the Grand Hotel, a very impressive edifice built in the French Renaissance style and opened in 1901.

HARTLEPOOL, THE MUNICIPAL BUILDINGS 1901 47978

HARTLEPOOL
The Municipal Buildings 1901

Situated in what is now Church Square, the offices of the council were all accommodated in a very distinctive building built in the Queen Anne style. It was opened in 1889 by HRH Prince Albert Victor, who was the first member of the Royal Family to perform an official ceremony in Hartlepool. The building was on top of the large quarry from which limestone had been taken for the building of Christ Church.

◆

HARTLEPOOL
Christ Church 1913

Christ Church stands at the top of Church Street; it was built in 1854 and paid for by Ralph Ward Jackson, a famous patron of the town. His statue can be seen here. The ground and limestone were donated by the Dock Company, but the remaining costs were still well over £6,000. The altar rails were made of bog oak excavated from the submerged forest. In recent years the church has been renovated; it is now the Tourist Information Centre and Hartlepool

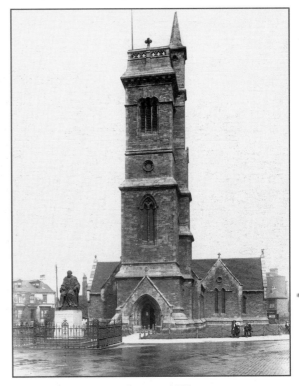

HARTLEPOOL, CHRIST CHURCH 1913 66418

HARTLEPOOL, ST JAMES'S CHURCH 1886 18855
The church stood on the corner of Musgrave Street and Whitby Street. It was opened and consecrated in 1869. In 1956 it was decided to build a church of the same name in Owton Manor, a suburb of Hartlepool. The original church was then demolished.

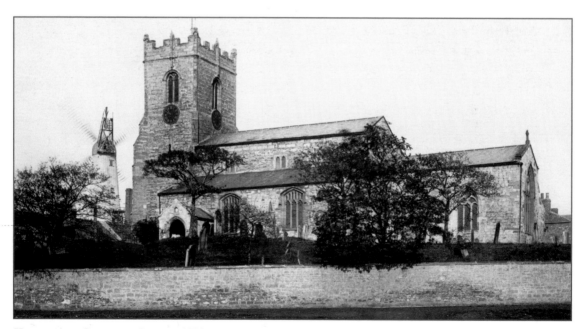

HARTLEPOOL, STRANTON CHURCH 1886 18863
All Saints Church dates back to 1129. A parson here in the 17th century was recorded to have herded several couples that were to be married up the aisle. In the middle of the service, one bridegroom shouted that he had the wrong lass beside him; the others then shouted the same. The parson answered with 'Hush, have ye no reverence in the House of God? Stay where you are till I'm finished and sort yourselves out later'!

Index

Frith Book Co Titles

www.frithbook.co.uk

The Frith Book Company publishes over 100 new titles each year. A selection of those currently available are listed below. For latest catalogue please contact Frith Book Co.

Town Books 96pp, 100 photos. County and Themed Books 128pp, 150 photos (unless specified). All titles hardback laminated case and jacket except those indicated pb (paperback)

Around Bakewell	1-85937-113-2	£12.99	English Castles	1-85937-078-0	£14.99
Around Barnstaple	1-85937-084-5	£12.99	Essex	1-85937-082-9	£14.99
Around Bath	1-85937-097-7	£12.99	Around Exeter	1-85937-126-4	£12.99
Around Belfast	1-85937-094-2	£12.99	Exmoor	1-85937-132-9	£14.99
Berkshire (pb)	1-85937-191-4	£9.99	Around Falmouth	1-85937-066-7	£12.99
Around Blackpool	1-85937-049-7	£12.99	Around Great Yarmouth	1-85937-085-3	£12.99
Around Bognor Regis	1-85937-055-1	£12.99	Greater Manchester	1-85937-108-6	£14.99
Around Bournemouth	1-85937-067-5	£12.99	Around Guildford	1-85937-117-5	£12.99
Brighton (pb)	1-85937-192-2	£8.99	Hampshire	1-85937-064-0	£14.99
Around Bristol	1-85937-050-0	£12.99	Around Harrogate	1-85937-112-4	£12.99
British Life A Century Ago	1-85937-103-5	£17.99	Around Horsham	1-85937-127-2	£12.99
Buckinghamshire (pb)	1-85937-200-7	£9.99	Around Ipswich	1-85937-133-7	£12.99
Around Cambridge	1-85937-092-6	£12.99	Ireland (pb)	1-85937-181-7	£9.99
Cambridgeshire	1-85937-086-1	£14.99	Isle of Man	1-85937-065-9	£14.99
Canals and Waterways	1-85937-129-9	£17.99	Isle of Wight	1-85937-114-0	£14.99
Cheshire	1-85937-045-4	£14.99	Kent (pb)	1-85937-189-2	£9.99
Around Chester	1-85937-090-x	£12.99	Around Leicester	1-85937-073-x	£12.99
Around Chesterfield	1-85937-071-3	£12.99	Leicestershire (pb)	1-85937-185-x	£9.99
Around Chichester	1-85937-089-6	£12.99	Around Lincoln	1-85937-111-6	£12.99
Churches of Berkshire	1-85937-170-1	£17.99	Lincolnshire	1-85937-135-3	£14.99
Churches of Dorset	1-85937-172-8	£17.99	Around Liverpool	1-85937-051-9	£12.99
Colchester (pb)	1-85937-188-4	£8.99	London (pb)	1-85937-183-3	£9.99
Cornwall	1-85937-054-3	£14.99	Around Maidstone	1-85937-056-x	£12.99
Cotswolds	1-85937-099-3	£14.99	New Forest	1-85937-128-0	£14.99
Cumbria	1-85937-101-9	£14.99	Around Newark	1-85937-105-1	£12.99
Dartmoor	1-85937-145-0	£14.99	Around Newquay	1-85937-140-x	£12.99
Around Derby	1-85937-046-2	£12.99	North Devon Coast	1-85937-146-9	£14.99
Derbyshire (pb)	1-85937-196-5	£9.99	North Yorkshire	1-85937-048-9	£14.99
Devon	1-85937-052-7	£14.99	Northumberland and Tyne & Wear		
Dorset	1-85937-075-6	£14.99		1-85937-072-1	£14.99
Dorset Coast	1-85937-062-4	£14.99	Norwich (pb)	1-85937-194-9	£8.99
Down the Severn	1-85937-118-3	£14.99	Around Nottingham	1-85937-060-8	£12.99
Down the Thames	1-85937-121-3	£14.99	Nottinghamshire (pb)	1-85937-187-6	£9.99
Around Dublin	1-85937-058-6	£12.99	Around Oxford	1-85937-096-9	£12.99
East Anglia	1-85937-059-4	£14.99	Oxfordshire	1-85937-076-4	£14.99
East Sussex	1-85937-130-2	£14.99	Peak District	1-85937-100-0	£14.99
Around Eastbourne	1-85937-061-6	£12.99	Around Penzance	1-85937-069-1	£12.99
Edinburgh (pb)	1-85937-193-0	£8.99	Around Plymouth	1-85937-119-1	£12.99

Available from your local bookshop or from the publisher

Frith Book Co Titles (continued)

Around Reading	1-85937-087-x	£12.99		Stone Circles & Ancient Monuments		
Redhill to Reigate	1-85937-137-x	£12.99			1-85937-143-4	£17.99
Around St Ives	1-85937-068-3	£12.99		Around Stratford upon Avon		
Around Salisbury	1-85937-091-8	£12.99			1-85937-098-5	£12.99
Around Scarborough	1-85937-104-3	£12.99		Suffolk	1-85937-074-8	£14.99
Scotland (pb)	1-85937-182-5	£9.99		Sussex (pb)	1-85937-184-1	£9.99
Scottish Castles	1-85937-077-2	£14.99		Surrey	1-85937-081-0	£14.99
Around Sevenoaks and Tonbridge				Around Torbay	1-85937-063-2	£12.99
	1-85937-057-8	£12.99		Around Truro	1-85937-147-7	£12.99
Sheffield and S Yorkshire	1-85937-070-5	£14.99		Victorian & Edwardian Kent		
Around Southampton	1-85937-088-8	£12.99			1-85937-149-3	£14.99
Around Southport	1-85937-106-x	£12.99		Victorian & Edwardian Yorkshire		
Around Shrewsbury	1-85937-110-8	£12.99			1-85937-154-x	£14.99
Shropshire	1-85937-083-7	£14.99		Warwickshire (pb)	1-85937-203-1	£9.99
South Devon Coast	1-85937-107-8	£14.99		Welsh Castles	1-85937-120-5	£14.99
South Devon Living Memories				West Midlands	1-85937-109-4	£14.99
	1-85937-168-x	£14.99		West Sussex	1-85937-148-5	£14.99
Staffordshire (96pp)	1-85937-047-0	£12.99		Wiltshire	1-85937-053-5	£14.99
				Around Winchester	1-85937-139-6	£12.99

Frith Book Co titles available Autumn 2000

Croydon Living Memories (pb)					Worcestershire	1-85937-152-3	£14.99	Sep
	1-85937-162-0	£9.99	Aug		Yorkshire Living Memories	1-85937-166-3	£14.99	Sep
Glasgow (pb)	1-85937-190-6	£9.99	Aug					
Hertfordshire (pb)	1-85937-247-3	£9.99	Aug		British Life A Century Ago (pb)			
North London	1-85937-206-6	£14.99	Aug			1-85937-213-9	£9.99	Oct
Victorian & Edwardian Maritime Album					Camberley (pb)	1-85937-222-8	£9.99	Oct
	1-85937-144-2	£17.99	Aug		Cardiff (pb)	1-85937-093-4	£9.99	Oct
Victorian Seaside	1-85937-159-0	£17.99	Aug		Carmarthenshire	1-85937-216-3	£14.99	Oct
					Cornwall (pb)	1-85937-229-5	£9.99	Oct
Cornish Coast	1-85937-163-9	£14.99	Sep		English Country Houses	1-85937-161-2	£17.99	Oct
County Durham	1-85937-123-x	£14.99	Sep		Humberside	1-85937-215-5	£14.99	Oct
Dorset Living Memories	1-85937-210-4	£14.99	Sep		Lancashire (pb)	1-85937-197-3	£9.99	Oct
Gloucestershire	1-85937-102-7	£14.99	Sep		Liverpool (pb)	1-85937-234-1	£9.99	Oct
Herefordshire	1-85937-174-4	£14.99	Sep		Manchester (pb)	1-85937-198-1	£9.99	Oct
Kent Living Memories	1-85937-125-6	£14.99	Sep		Middlesex	1-85937-158-2	£14.99	Oct
Leeds (pb)	1-85937-202-3	£9.99	Sep		Norfolk Living Memories	1-85937-217-1	£14.99	Oct
Ludlow (pb)	1-85937-176-0	£9.99	Sep		Preston (pb)	1-85937-212-0	£9.99	Oct
Norfolk (pb)	1-85937-195-7	£9.99	Sep		South Hams	1-85937-220-1	£14.99	Oct
Somerset	1-85937-153-1	£14.99	Sep		Suffolk	1-85937-221-x	£9.99	Oct
Tees Valley & Cleveland	1-85937-211-2	£14.99	Sep		Swansea (pb)	1-85937-167-1	£9.99	Oct
Thanet (pb)	1-85937-116-7	£9.99	Sep		Victorian and Edwardian Sussex			
Tiverton (pb)	1-85937-178-7	£9.99	Sep			1-85937-157-4	£14.99	Oct
Weymouth (pb)	1-85937-209-0	£9.99	Sep		West Yorkshire (pb)	1-85937-201-5	£9.99	Oct

See Frith books on the internet www.frithbook.co.uk

FRITH PRODUCTS & SERVICES

Francis Frith would doubtless be pleased to know that the pioneering publishing venture he started in 1860 still continues today. A hundred and forty years later, The Francis Frith Collection continues in the same innovative tradition and is now one of the foremost publishers of vintage photographs in the world. Some of the current activities include:

Interior Decoration

Today Frith's photographs can be seen framed and as giant wall murals in thousands of pubs, restaurants, hotels, banks, retail stores and other public buildings throughout the country. In every case they enhance the unique local atmosphere of the places they depict and provide reminders of gentler days in an increasingly busy and frenetic world.

Product Promotions

Frith products are used by many major companies to promote the sales of their own products or to reinforce their own history and heritage. Frith promotions have been used by Hovis bread, Courage beers, Scots Porage Oats, Colman's mustard, Cadbury's foods, Mellow Birds coffee, Dunhill pipe tobacco, Guinness, and Bulmer's Cider.

Genealogy and Family History

As the interest in family history and roots grows world-wide, more and more people are turning to Frith's photographs of Great Britain for images of the towns, villages and streets where their ancestors lived; and, of course, photographs of the churches and chapels where their ancestors were christened, married and buried are an essential part of every genealogy tree and family album.

Frith Products

All Frith photographs are available Framed or just as Mounted Prints and Posters (size 23 x 16 inches). These may be ordered from the address below. From time to time other products - Address Books, Calendars, Table Mats, etc - are available.

The Internet

Already twenty thousand Frith photographs can be viewed and purchased on the internet. By the end of the year 2000 some 60,000 Frith photographs will be available on the internet. The number of sites is constantly expanding, each focussing on different products and services from the Collection.
The main Frith sites are listed below.
www.francisfrith.co.uk
www.frithbook.co.uk

See the complete list of Frith Books at:
www.frithbook.co.uk
This web site is regularly updated with the latest list of publications from the Frith Book Company. If you wish to buy books relating to another part of the country that your local bookshop does not stock, you may purchase on-line.

For further information, trade, or author enquiries please contact us at the address below:
The Francis Frith Collection, Frith's Barn, Teffont, Salisbury, Wiltshire, England SP3 5QP.
Tel: +44 (0)1722 716 376 Fax: +44 (0)1722 716 881 Email: uksales@francisfrith.com

See Frith books on the internet www.frithbook.co.uk